A Guide to English Academic Writing for Beginners

Akira Tajino

Sayako Maswana
Yoshitaka Kato
Hironori Watari
Hiroshi Yamada

Asahi Press

はしがき

　本書は、パラグラフライティングを学ぶことを通してEGP（一般目的の英語）からEAP（学術目的の英語）への橋渡しを目指しています。読み手に伝わる英語を書くためには、英語の文章作成の基本となるパラグラフライティングのルールや構成に習熟しておく必要があります。和文英訳など「英作文」を学んできた学生が、さらに一歩進んで、まとまりのある文章を書くためには、パラグラフライティングは有効な方法です。書くことを通して、学生は思考を整理し、自分なりの意見を形作ることができるようになります。本書では、モデルとなるパラグラフの読解、語彙問題、文法問題、ブレーンストーミング、図や表を使ったライティングタスクと、豊富な練習を通して、パラグラフライティングの書き方にとどまらず、段階的に英語の総合力を高められるように工夫しました。また、1文レベルでも英語を書くことに抵抗感をもっている学生にも配慮し、英語の語順を習得できる「意味順」学習法も紹介しています（詳しくは田地野 (2011)「〈意味順〉英作文のすすめ」（岩波書店）などをご参照ください）。

　本書は、以下のように15週で利用できるように構成されています。

[モデルプラン]

Week 1	Unit 1: Introduction	Week 9	Unit 4: Cause / Effect Paragraph
Week 2		Week 10	
Week 3	Unit 2: Narrative / Descriptive Paragraph	Week 11	Unit 5: Opinion Paragraph
Week 4		Week 12	
Week 5		Week 13	
Week 6	Unit 3: Comparison / Contrast Paragraph	Week 14	Unit 6: Toward Writing a 300-Word Essay
Week 7		Week 15	
Week 8			

　Introductionでパラグラフと英文作成の基礎を学んだのち、四つの代表的なパラグラフの型を、それぞれ3回に分けてしっかりと学びます。最終週では、次の段階であるエッセイへの導入を学ぶことができます。本書では、学生たちに親しみやすいトピックを選び、スピーキング活動やピアフィードバックなどのペアワークも取り入れています。本書を通して達成するCan-Doリストも次ページに示しています。CEFR-Jに準拠したリストですので、どのような力が身に着くか、具体的に把握することが可能です。

　英語のライティングにはパラグラフという型は存在しますが、表現の方法は幾通りも可能です。パラグラフという型を土台として、自由な発想を発展させ、コミュニケーションを楽しんでもらえれば幸いです。

2019年7月　監修者　田地野 彰

— Can-Do Statements —
●

Listening
- ゆっくり丁寧に話されれば、何について話されているか理解することができる。(A2)

Reading
- 簡単な言葉で書かれた文章なら、よく知っているトピックを扱った日常的な事柄についての短い物語を理解することができる。(A2)
- 簡単な文章の中の特定の情報を見つけることができる。(A2)
- 基礎的な日常語を含む自分と関係のある、あるいは自分が関心のある分野に関する短い簡単なメッセージや文章を理解することができる。(A2)
- 物語や出来事を詳しく記述している新聞・雑誌の短い報告の中の重要な情報を理解することができる。(A2)
- 構成がはっきりとした物語の筋を理解することができる。(B1)
- はっきりと書かれた論説文の主な結論を理解することができる。(B1)

Spoken Interaction
- 簡単な質問をしたり、簡単な質問に答えることができる。また、必要性の高いことや身近な話題について発言したり、反応することができる。(A1)
- 相手が協力的であれば短い社会的なやり取りができ、理解させることができる。(A2)
- 普段の状況で興味がある話題であれば短い会話に参加することができる。(A2)
- 好きなことや嫌いなことを話したり、相手に賛成したり反対したり、比較することができる。(A2)
- 週末の予定などを話し合うことができる。(A2)

Spoken Production
- 自分の教育的な背景や専門分野を説明することができる。(A2)
- 先週末の出来事、直近の休日の出来事など過去の活動や経験を説明することができる。(A2)
- 普段することを説明することができる。(A2)

Writing
- ある出来事について短く記述することができる。(A2)
- "and", "but", "because"のような語でつなげながら、簡単な文を書くことができる。(A2)
- "and", "but", "then"を使って、簡単な文をつないでより長い文にすることができる。(A2)
- 日常生活のさまざまな面を簡単な句や文で書くことができる（例：家族、学校、趣味、休日、好き嫌い）。(A2)
- 自分の関心がある分野のさまざまなトピックについて、簡単なつながりのある文

章を書くことができる。(B1)

● 身近なトピックについての事実情報の簡単な要約を書くことができる。(B1)

● 過去に起こったことについて述べる簡単な物語を書くことができる。(B1)

● 短い個々の語句をつなぎ合わせて並べ、また辞書や参考資料を使って、簡単なつながりのある文章や簡単なエッセイを書くことができる。(B1)

● 賛成、反対を比較検討しながら、ある視点を支持する、あるいは否定する意見を述べて、議論を展開するエッセイや報告を書くことができる。(B2)

「ELP Can Do Descriptor Database」(2013) 東京外国語大学投野由紀夫研究室. http://www.cefr-j.org/data/CanDoDescriptorBook1.0.pdf

目 次

WEEK

1 **Unit 1** Introduction — Lesson 1 —— 2

2 Lesson 2 —— 7

3 **Unit 2** Narrative / Descriptive Paragraph — Lesson 1 —— 14

4 Lesson 2 —— 18

5 Lesson 3 —— 22

6 **Unit 3** Comparison / Contrast Paragraph — Lesson 1 —— 28

7 Lesson 2 —— 32

8 Lesson 3 —— 36

9 **Unit 4** Cause / Effect Paragraph — Lesson 1 —— 42

10 Lesson 2 —— 47

11 Lesson 3 —— 51

12 **Unit 5** Opinion Paragraph — Lesson 1 —— 56

13 Lesson 2 —— 60

14 Lesson 3 —— 64

15 **Unit 6** Toward Writing a 300-Word Essay —— 70

Unit 1

Introduction

アカデミックライティングとは ―EGPからEAPへ―

　高校と大学では、英語ライティングにも違いがあります。高校までの英語ライティングは、一文の文法的な正確さが重視される和文英訳や、好きな食べ物や印象に残った出来事などをトピックとして主観的な感想を書く自由英作文が多かったと思います。一方、大学では、レポート課題や論文など、客観的に事実を述べ、資料を用いながら意見を論理的に組み立てることが必要となってきます。大学では、「書かれたもの」が評価の対象となることが多く、ライティングの知識や技能は授業の単位を取ることにとどまらず、アカデミック・コミュニケーションの重要なスキルです。この点においては、英語と日本語のライティングに変わりはありません。

　専門用語で高校までの英語はEGP (English for General Purposes：一般目的の英語)、学問や研究に関わる人たちが使う英語はEAP (English for Academic Purposes: 学術目的の英語) と呼ばれています。本書は、EAPライティングの基礎となる「パラグラフライティング」を学ぶことにより、EGPからEAPの橋渡しをすることを目指しています。

パラグラフとは

　日本語の段落とは少し異なり、パラグラフには一定の書き方が存在しています。第一として、一つのパラグラフでは一つのアイディアしか書くことはできません。また、やみくもにトピックに関連する文章を書くのではなく、読み手に伝わりやすい順序で書きます。

1. 以下の文章を見てみましょう。何のことが書かれているか考えてみましょう。

　　新聞の方が雑誌よりいい。街中より海岸の方が場所としていい。最初は歩くより走る方がいい。何度もトライしなくてはならないだろう。ちょっとしたコツがいるが、つかむのは易しい。小さな子どもでも楽しめる。一度成功すると面倒は少ない。鳥が近づきすぎることはめったにない。ただ、雨はすぐしみ込む。多すぎる人がこれをいっせいにやると面倒がおきうる。ひとつについてかなりのスペースがいる。面倒がなければ、のどかなものである。石はアンカーがわりに使える。ゆるんでものがとれたりすると、それで終わりである。

（西林克彦 (2005)「わかったつもり 読解力がつかない本当の原因」光文社 p.45）

　おそらく、多くの人が分かりにくい文章だと思ったでしょう。この文章が分かりにくかった理由は、最初に何の話なのか書かれていなかったことが一番の原因です。特にパラグラフでは、最初に「トピックセンテンス」という、そのパラグラフで最も言いたいことをまとめた文を書く必要があります。その後にサポーティングセンテンス（支持文）というトピックセンテンスを支える文を書き、コンクルーディングセンテンス（結論文）というトピック

センテンスを言い換えてパラグラフをまとめる文を書きます。要するに、最初にこれから説明する内容を一文で表し、実際に内容を説明し、最後に何を言ったかまとめる、という順序がパラグラフの基本となります。確かに、この順序でしたら伝えたい内容が伝わりやすいでしょう。この順序を視覚的にとらえて、ハンバーガーライティングと表現することもあります。

相手に伝わるように書くのは書き手の責任であり、読み手を常に意識することが必要です。

2. 以下の文を理解し、読みやすいパラグラフとなるように文の順番を書きましょう。

● The importance of water ●

___1___ Water plays important roles in the human body and agriculture.

_____ Next, water is also necessary for growing plants and vegetables.

_____ First, a significant amount of water supports the body's functioning.

_____ Technology has been developed in many places to provide water for agriculture.

_____ In conclusion, water is critical for our health and our lives.

_____ It is demonstrated by the fact that we feel sick when our bodies become dehydrated during the summer.

　上のパラグラフの第1文がトピックセンテンスです。このパラグラフにあるように、First（第一に）やIn conclusion（結論として）など、パラグラフ内で順序を示す表現が存在します。多くの場合、表現のあとにコンマ (,) が入ります。また、語彙も日常会話で使われる平易なものから、develop（発展する）やit is demonstrated〜（〜が示される）など、アカデミックな文脈で汎用性のある表現を使うことが求められます。

◉◉◉ 良いパラグラフとは ◉◉◉

　良いパラグラフとは、一文の文法的な正確さはもちろんのこと、上のトピックセンテンス・支持文・結論文を持つことに加えて、結束性（coherence）と一貫性（consistency）が備わっているものです。結束性とは、それぞれの文が互いにスムーズにつながっていることを指します。また、一貫性とは、すべての文がトピックセンテンスに関連していることを指します。

3. 以下のパラグラフを読み、トピックセンテンスに関連していない文を指摘しましょう。

Successful athletes

[1] The keys to success as an athlete are consistent, hard practice and mental strength. [2] Successful athletes practice more than their peers to excel at their sports. [3] Many athletes have physical strength and athletic ability, so the difference between athletes is whether they make consistent efforts to improve. [4] It is very expensive to buy sports gear. [5] Additionally, they must be mentally strong to be successful. [6] Athletes often face difficult times, but those who succeed are not discouraged by challenges and instead learn from them. [7] Practice and mental capacity are important factors for athletes.

●●● いろいろなパラグラフ ●●●

パラグラフにはいろいろなタイプがあり、例えばNarrative（物語）、Description（描写）、Exposition（説明：その中に比較、原因・影響などを含む）、Argumentation（意見）があります。トピックセンテンス・支持文・結論文からなるという大きな型は変わりませんが、支持文の中身や特徴的な表現が変わってきます。本書では、大学で用いられることの多い4つの代表的なパラグラフ（Narrative / Descriptive, Comparison / Contrast, Cause / Effect, Opinion）の書き方を学びます。

4. 以下の空欄に入る適切な語を、下のComparison / Contrast（比較）パラグラフで多く用いられる表現から選びましょう。

1) _____ high school students, university students can decide what classes to take.

（高校生とは異なり、大学生は受講する授業を決めることができる。）

2) _____ vitamins, protein is crucial for the human body.

（ビタミンと同様に、たんぱく質は人間の体に欠かせない。）

> 類似を示す：similarity, also, both, like
> 異なりを示す：in contrast, on the other hand, whereas, while, unlike

◉◉◉ 類義語 ◉◉◉

　英語ライティングでは、キーワードは繰り返しますが、同じ言葉を何度も繰り返すことは好まれないため、類義語 (synonym) を用いることがあります。多様な語彙を使いこなすことは、EAP ライティングで重要となります。

5. 下の語の類義語を考えてみましょう。類語辞典 (thesaurus) が参考になります。

　　1) support: _____ , _____

　　2) sick: _____ , _____

　　3) important: _____ , _____

　　4) quick: _____ , _____

◉◉◉ 言い換え ◉◉◉

　英語ライティングでは、「言い換え (paraphrase)」は重要なスキルの一つです。パラグラフでは、結論文は多くの場合、トピックセンテンスを言い換えたものとなります。言い換えは、原文と同じ内容を自分の言葉で表現することです。上に挙げた類義語を使って単語を置き換えるだけではなく、文の構造も変えることが推奨されています。ここで言い換えの練習をしてみましょう。

　　　　悪い例: I love this song. ⇒ I like this song.
　　　　良い例: I love this song. ⇒ This is my favorite song.

　良い例では、言っている内容は同じでも主語が変わっています。

6. 下の文を言い換えてみましょう。

　　1) He is good at playing tennis.

　　　⇒ _____

　　2) I cannot sleep if I drink coffee.

　　　⇒ _____

●●● ライティングのプロセス ●●●

　ライティングは、一連のプロセスを経て行われます。大きく分けて、「アイディアの発見」
→「アウトラインとドラフトの作成」→「見直し」→「最終版の作成」です。それぞれのステップには、いろいろな方法があります。例えば「アイディアの発見」ですが、以下のようにトピックを中心として、それに関連したものを蜘蛛の巣のようにつなげていく方法もその一つです。多くのアイディアが出たところで、どのような内容をどう書くかを考えます。

7. トピック「日本文化」に関連するものを、下に書き出しましょう。

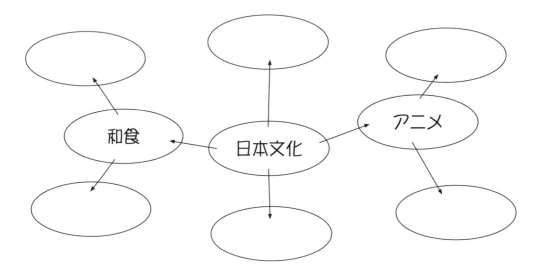

Unit 1 ・ Lesson 2

【 まず一文を書く 】

　本書の目標であるまとまりのある論理的なパラグラフを書くために、まず英語で一文を書く方法を見直しておく必要があります。ここでは、英語と日本語の違いに注目しながら英語における語順の重要性を確認したのち、英文ライティングを助ける「意味順」英作文の考えを紹介します。

●●● 英語のからくり ― 語順の大切さ ●●●

> a. Tom had fish and chips.
>
> b. Fish and chips had Tom.

1. aとbの文の言語的な違いは何でしょう。

2. aとbの文は、どちらが自然な文でしょうか。

　私たちが学んでいる英語は、どのような言語的特徴を持っているのでしょうか。上の例からも分かるように、英語には「語順が変わると意味が変わる」という特徴があります。では、日本語の場合はどうでしょうか。

> c. 太郎がハンバーガーを食べた。
>
> d. ハンバーガーを太郎が食べた。

3. cとdの文の言語的な違いは何でしょう。

4. cとdの文は、どちらが自然な文でしょうか。

　上の例からも分かるように、助詞（「を」や「が」など）の機能に支えられている日本語では、語順が変わっても英語ほどには意味が変わりません。

●●● 「良い間違い」と「悪い間違い」 ●●●

> e. I have some cofee yesterday night and can't sleep wel.
>
> f. Last week the zoo went and an elephant saw.

5. eとfの文の「間違い」を指摘してみましょう。

6. eとfの文は、どちらが理解可能な文でしょうか。

7. eとfの文を修正するとすれば、どのような文になるでしょうか？

　もちろん完璧な文章を書けることに越したことはありませんが、外国語である英語で文

を書くという作業は簡単ではなく、どんなに優れた言語使用者でも時には間違えることがあります。ただし、そうした「間違い」をコミュニケーションの観点から考えた時、意味が伝わる「良い間違い」と意味が伝わらない「悪い間違い」があるのは事実です。文脈にも影響されるために一概に区分することはできませんが、スペルや冠詞などの間違いに比べて、語順の間違いは英文の意味に大きな影響を与えやすい要素であると言えるでしょう。では、自然な英語の語順で書くにはどうすればよいのでしょうか。

◉◉◉ シンプルな語順の原則 ─ 意味順 ◉◉◉

ここでは、英語ライティングを始めるにあたり、英語の語順の原則を簡潔に説明した「意味順」を紹介します。

意味順 (= 英語の語順)

> 「だれが」「する（です）」「だれ・なに」「どこ」「いつ」

オプション：「α」、「どのように (して)」、「なぜ」

この意味順さえ頭に入れておけば、誰でも英語の意味のまとまりごとに自然な文を書くことができ、例えばf.のように、理解困難な英文を書いてしまうことが圧倒的に少なくなります。

以下の表は、Unit 1 Lesson 1の文章 (Successful athletes) を意味順の枠に沿って整理したものです。

	α	だれが	する (です)	だれ・なに	どこ、いつ、どのように(して)、なぜ	
1		The keys to success as an athlete	are	consistent, hard practice and mental strength.		
2		Successful athletes	practice		more than their peers	to excel at their sports.
3		Many athletes	have	physical strength and athletic ability,		
	so	the difference between athletes	is			
	whether	they	make	consistent efforts	to improve.	

5	Additionally,	they	must be	mentally strong	to be successful.	
6		Athletes	ofren face	difficult times,		
	but	those who succeed	are not discouraged	by challenges		
	and instead		learn		from them.	
7		Practice and mental capacity	are	important factors for athletes.		

8. 上の表の中で何か疑問に思う点はありますか？

　ここでの英語学習の目標は「英文を整理する」ことではなく、あくまで「英文を書く」ことですから、上の表の細かな点については気にする必要はありません。ここでは、以下の2つの原則について感覚的に理解することが大切です。

(A) 英語の文(節)は、意味順に沿って作られる。
(B) 英語の文(節)は、「だれが」「する(です)」の要素を含む。

　(A) に関しては、表の英文が原則的に意味順枠に沿って左から右に流れていることから明らかです。(B) に関しては、一部「だれが」が文脈上明らかなために省略されている箇所 (表の下から2行目) がありますが、原則的にすべての文 (や節) が「だれが」「する(です)」の要素を含んでいることが見て取れます。日本語では「だれが」の要素を省略することも多いのですが、表ではthey (つまり successful athletes) という表現が何度も使われていることが分かりますね。

9. 次の2文をそれぞれ以下の枠に入れてみましょう。

1. I went to the zoo last week and saw an elephant.
2. The line graph shows the number of books that were borrowed in this library last year.

	α	だれが	する (です)	だれ・なに	どこ、いつ、どのように(して)、なぜ
1					
2					

◆◆◆ 「英語にしやすい日本語」の発想 ◆◆◆

　日本語に比べて使える表現（語彙や文法）が限られている英語では、自分の考えや思いを英語で伝えることは容易ではありません。その点において、意味順は私たちの日本語発想を英語発想に切り替える作業を非常にスムーズにしてくれます。英語の文を書くポイントは、「英語にしやすい日本語」を発想することです。例えば、「コーヒーを飲むと寝られない。」と言いたい時に、Coffee から文を始めるとその先の言葉に詰まってしまうことがよくあります。英文ライティングで重要なのは、「だれが」の要素を柔軟に変えることです。以下のように、もし I から文を始めれば、英語にしやすい日本語に噛み砕くことができるはずです。

「コーヒーを飲むと寝られない。」

→ コーヒーは...

→ Coffee　眠れなくする　私を　??

→ 私は　眠れない　もし　私が　飲む　コーヒーを

→ I cannot sleep if I drink coffee.

　もちろん Lesson 1 の言い換え（paraphrase）で触れたように、上級者になるにつれて様々な表現の引き出しが増えるため、Coffee を「だれが」に定めても Coffee keeps me awake. のような英語らしい表現ができることでしょう。この上級レベルを片隅で意識しながらも、意味順の枠を用いながら、自分が現在もっている表現の中で柔軟に発想していくことが大切です。

Writing exercise

以下の日本語を英語にしてみましょう。

・あえて英語にしづらい日本語文を問題にしています。

・解答は1つではありません。柔軟に発想してみましょう。

1. 料理がうまいね。

2. 朝のカレーは元気が出る。

3. キリン (the giraffe) は首が長い。

4. 喫煙は健康に良くない。

5. その結果は悪くないと思うよ。

6. ご覧の通り、子どもの数は少ない。

7. 2つの理由からその意見に賛成である。

8. その問題を解決するのは容易でない。

9. 若者の多くが将来に不安を抱えている。

10. その計画には大きな問題がある。

Unit 2

Narrative / Descriptive Paragraph

▌ What's a Narrative Paragraph? ▐

Narrative Paragraph：ある［　　　　］について語る

● 使用例：日記、新聞記事、［　　　　］、伝記など

● 言語的特徴：［　　　　］に沿って書かれる。動詞は［　　　　］が使われることが多い。

1. 最も適切な語を挿入し、上の説明を完成させましょう。

   矛盾　　出来事　　メモ　　小説　　時系列　　主張　　現在形　　過去形

2. Narrative を日本語で何と言うでしょうか。

◆ **Warm-up questions** ◆

1. What did you do last weekend?

2. Have you ever been abroad?

3. What country would you like to go?

■■■　　　Model paragraph 1　　　■■■

Title

Last week, I went to Edinburgh, the capital city of Scotland. The city was very beautiful except for one thing: the loud and noisy sound I could hear in the city. At first, I couldn't identify the source of the uncomfortable sound, but soon I realized that it was a bagpipe, Scotland's traditional woodwind instrument. I found many bagpipe players on the streets during the trip, and oddly enough, I got used to the sound and even liked it in the end! Now, I am back in Japan, listening to bagpipe music online. We cannot tell what will happen to us tomorrow.

【内容理解】

1. Ken が書いた上の文章を読んで、True / False / Not given を選びましょう。

   ・Ken は昨年、エディンバラを旅行した。　　　　　　　　　　［　　　　　　　］

   ・騒音の原因は、スコットランドの伝統的な楽器だった。　　　［　　　　　　　］

・Kenは徐々にバグパイプの音を好むようになった。　　　[　　　　　　]

・Kenは時々、日本でバグパイプのコンサートに行っている。[　　　　　　]

2. この文章に、英単語5語以内で適切なタイトルをつけてみましょう。

【形式理解】

1. トピックセンテンスに下線を引きましょう。

2. 文章中の「時を表す表現（例：Last week）」を3つ□で囲みましょう。

3. まとめの文があれば波線を引きましょう。

■ ■ ■　Model paragraph 2　■ ■ ■

Mirrored face

The other day, a cat named Daisy (1)have a very shocking day. She was (2)cross a bridge in a good mood with a fish in her mouth. On the middle of the bridge, she (3)notice her mirrored face on the surface of the river. She (4)wonder who it was. Thinking that it might be her enemy, she (5)scream at her own face on the river. Then, she mistakenly (6)drop her fish in the river. She (7)is really shocked to lose her precious dinner.

1. 文章中の動詞（1）～（7）を適切な形に変化させ、文章を完成させましょう。

　(1) ＿＿＿＿＿＿　　(2) ＿＿＿＿＿＿　　(3) ＿＿＿＿＿＿　　(4) ＿＿＿＿＿＿

　(5) ＿＿＿＿＿＿　　(6) ＿＿＿＿＿＿　　(7) ＿＿＿＿＿＿

2. What do you think Daisy did next? Imagine the story and add another sentence at the end.

以下の意味を表す単語を選び、（　　）に書きましょう。

1. (　　　　　　　　　): valuable or important and not to be wasted
2. (　　　　　　　　　): to understand or become aware of a particular fact
3. (　　　　　　　　　): to go or stretch from one side of something to the other
4. (　　　　　　　　　): the top layer of an area of water or land
5. (　　　　　　　　　): in a way that is wrong
6. (　　　　　　　　　): to recognize and correctly name someone or something
7. (　　　　　　　　　): a town or city of a country with primary status
8. (　　　　　　　　　): to think about something that you are not sure about
9. (　　　　　　　　　): an object used for producing music
10. (　　　　　　　　　): to not include something or someone

> wonder, except, mistakenly, instrument, precious, realize, surface, cross, capital, identify

1. 以下の表を完成させましょう。

	日本語	英語		日本語	英語
1	昨年		6	ある日	
2	昨夜		7	最初は	
3	午後 3 時に		8	最後に	
4	1997 年から		9	後で	
5	3 日間		10	その週の間	

2. 時制に気を付けながら、以下の日本文に合う英文を書きましょう。

(1) 私は昨夜、朝の2時に寝ました。

(2) 私は8年間英語を学んできました。

(3) その期間、お店は閉まる予定です。

Writing exercise

イラストは昨日の午後の様子です。イラスト中の人物が行っていたことを英語で描写しましょう。

[Picture 1]

·

·

·

·

·

[Picture 2]

·

·

·

·

·

What's a Descriptive Paragraph?

Descriptive Paragraph：情報などを [   ] する

● 使用例：[   ] や人物の説明など

● 言語的特徴：[   ] な事実を述べるため、[   ] や受動態が使われることが多い。

1. 適切な語を挿入し、上の説明を完成させましょう。

   イラスト化 描写 物語 図表 主観的 客観的 無生物主語 仮定法

2. Descriptiveを日本語で何と言うでしょうか。

◆ Warm-up questions ◆

1. What is the current population of Japan?

2. Is the Japanese population going to increase or decrease in the future? Why?

3. What energy resources do we depend on in Japan?

Model paragraph 1

日本の年齢階層別人口数推定（万人）
（World Population Prospects 2019より）

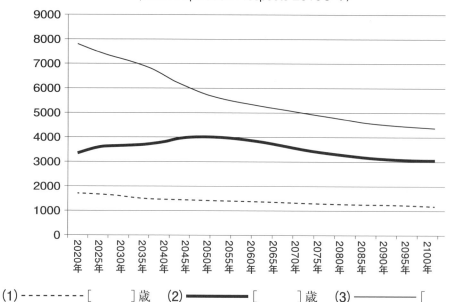

(1) - - - - - - - - [   ] 歳 (2) ━━━━ [   ] 歳 (3) ──── [   ] 歳

Estimated future population in Japan

This line graph shows how the population in Japan will change in the future. It specifically estimates the population change from 2020 to 2100 every five years. The dotted line indicates the number of people from 0 to 14 years old, the solid line from 15 to 64 and the thick line above 65. As you can see from this graph, the overall population in Japan is estimated to decrease gradually until 2100. The population of above 65 is going to reach the top in around 2045 and then gradually decrease while people less than 65 will constantly decrease in number.

【内容理解】

1. 上の文章を読んで、グラフの空欄（1）～（3）を埋めましょう。

【形式理解】

1. トピックセンテンスに下線を引きましょう。

2. 文章中の「グラフ説明に使える表現（例：This line graph shows…）」を3つ以上□で囲みましょう。

■■■　　Model paragraph 2　　■■■

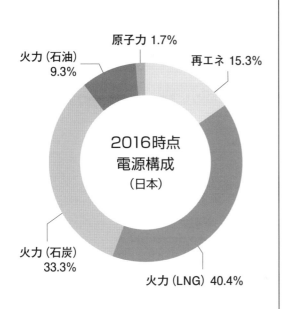

Title

This pie chart [1   ] the breakdown of the overall energy consumption in Japan in 2016. As you can see from the pie chart, thermal power generation is the main resource of Japanese energy. It [2   ] of natural gas, coal and oil power generation, and those energies in total [3   ] 83% of the overall. As other resources, renewable energy [4   ] for 15.3% while nuclear power generation 1.7%. This chart clearly shows our dependence on thermal power generation.

1. 以下の選択肢から空欄に入る適切な語を選び、文章を完成させましょう。

   [occupy, consists, shows, accounts]

2. この文章に英単語5語以内で適切なタイトルをつけてみましょう。

Vocabulary

以下の意味を表す単語を選び、（　　　）に書きましょう。

1. (　　　　　　　　): to be made up of two or more things or people
2. (　　　　　　　　): slowly, over a long period of time
3. (　　　　　　　　): to show
4. (　　　　　　　　): to rely on somebody / something
5. (　　　　　　　　): all the time, or very often
6. (　　　　　　　　): to fill a particular amount of space
7. (　　　　　　　　): in a detailed and exact way
8. (　　　　　　　　): to roughly judge the value, size, speed, cost etc. of
   something
9. (　　　　　　　　): a division into parts or categories
10. (　　　　　　　　): the act of using energy, food or materials

   [specifically, gradually, depend on, occupy, estimate, breakdown, consist of,
   consumption, constantly, indicate]

Grammar and expressions

1. 以下の表を完成させましょう。

	日本語	英語		日本語	英語
1	折れ線グラフ		6	太線	
2	円グラフ		7	点線	
3	棒グラフ		8	頂点に達する	
4	縦軸		9	最低に達する	
5	横軸		10	変化がない	

2. 以下の日本文に合う英文を書きましょう。

(1) 横軸は時間を表しています。

_____

(2) 人口は2000年から徐々に減少してきました。

_____

(3) 過去10年間、売上高に変化はありません。

_____

▪▪▪ ▪ Writing exercise ▪ ▪▪▪

以下のグラフはP.19 Model paragraph 2のグラフにある「再エネ」の内訳を示したものです。この円グラフを見て分かることを英語で3点描写してみましょう。

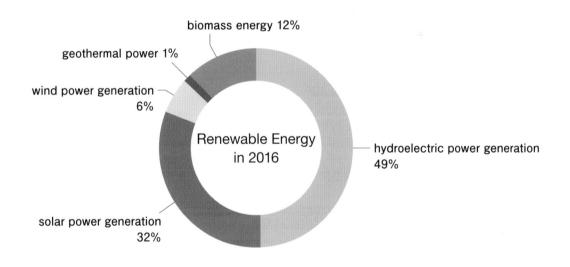

· _____

· _____

· _____

◆ **Warm-up questions** ◆

1. Do you know Emma Watson? How?
2. What are the differences of narrative and descriptive paragraphs?

■ ■ ■ Model paragraph ■ ■ ■

A short biography of Emma Watson

Emma Watson (born April 15, 1990) is an English actor and activist. She gained popularity at the age of nine when she appeared as Hermione Granger in the Harry Potter film series. More recently, she also acted the role of Belle in the film Beauty and the Beast released in 2017. Besides the job of actor, she is well-known for fighting actively for women's rights. In July 2014, she became a goodwill ambassador for UN Women and made an influential speech at the UN headquarters in New York. She constantly speaks of the importance of gender equality.

1. この文章は、narrative paragraph または descriptive paragraphのどちらでしょうか。
2. トピックセンテンスに下線を引きましょう。

■ ■ ■ Paragraph writing ■ ■ ■

以下の題材 (narrative/descriptive) のうち1つを選択し、パラグラフを書きましょう。

◆ **Narrative writing** ◆

Topic Look at the pictures and write a story. The woman is Susie and her son is Ted.

Brainstorm

イラストの吹き出しに入る会話文を日本語で自由に発想してみましょう。

(1) _____

(2) _____

(3) _____

Outline

パラグラフのアウトラインを作成しましょう。ここでは、会話文ではなく、場面を説明する文章を書きましょう。Unit 2のみトピックセンテンスがすでに書いてあります。

> トピックセンテンス： ある朝テッドが心配そうな顔をしていたので、母親が理由を聞いた。
>
> イラスト（1）： _____
>
> イラスト（2）： _____
>
> イラスト（3）： _____

● アウトラインをもとに、P. 25のYour paragraphを書きましょう。

Unit 2: L 3

◆ Descriptive writing ◆

Topic Write a descriptive paragraph about the bar graph below.

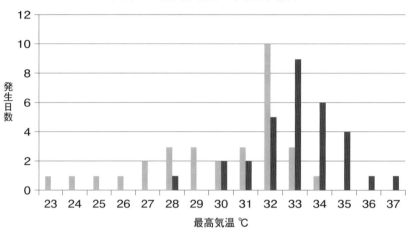

日本の最高気温の発生日数

凡例：
- ■ 1960年8月の最高気温の発生日数
- ■ 2010年8月の最高気温の発生日数

Brainstorm ●

上の棒グラフを見てわかるポイントを日本語で書いてみましょう。

Outline ●

パラグラフのアウトラインを作成しましょう。Unit 2のみトピックセンテンスがすでに書いてあります。

> トピックセンテンス： このグラフは、日本の8月の最高気温とその日数を示している。
>
> ポイント1：
>
> ポイント2：
>
> ポイント3：

● アウトラインをもとに、P. 25のYour paragraphを書きましょう。

Your paragraph

アウトラインをもとに、80語以上のパラグラフを書きましょう。

1. トピックセンテンスはありますか？　　「はい」・「いいえ」

2. どのようなポイントが書かれていますか？　すべて書いてみましょう。

   ・ _____

   ・ _____

3. つなぎの表現は入っていますか？

   「はい」→ 使われている表現を書いてみましょう。

   「いいえ」→ つなぎの表現を提案してみましょう。

   ・ _____

4. パラグラフの内容はすべて分かりましたか？

   「はい」

   「いいえ」→ どこが分かりませんでしたか？

   ・ _____

5. パラグラフの良い点を1つ挙げましょう。

   ・ _____

Revise ● 上のコメントをもとに、自分のパラグラフを修正しましょう。

Unit 3

Comparison / Contrast Paragraph

Unit 3 • Lesson 1

What's a Comparison / Contrast Paragraph?

Compare：ものごとの［　　　　］について語る。

Contrast：ものごとの［　　　　］について語る。

　ものごとを比較するときには「ものさし」をそろえる必要がある。飛行機と新幹線、どちらが速いかは、比較できる。しかし、飛行機とカップラーメン、どちらが速いかは比較しにくい。

［　　　　］に入る日本語を考えてみましょう。

◆ Warm-up questions ◆

1. What food do you like?
2. How many times a week do you go out for dinner?
3. What is your favorite restaurant or food shop?

Model paragraph 1

Apples and oranges

Apples and oranges have a lot of similarities. First, both are very popular fruits in Japan. People like to eat them for breakfast and dessert. Second, they are easy to eat. When you want to eat them, you only peel or cut them with a knife. Third, they are healthy and nutritious. They contain a lot of vitamins, minerals, and dietary fibers to maintain you in good shape and prevent diseases. Fourth, it is so easy to get them at a supermarket or even at a convenience store. These fruits are not so expensive and available all seasons. Fifth, they can be used in various dishes. You can make pies and cakes with apples and oranges. As above, apples and oranges have many things in common.

【内容理解】

1. リンゴとオレンジの共通点は（　　　　）個、挙げられている。

2. 共通点を整理してみましょう。

【形式理解】

1. トピックセンテンスに下線を引きましょう。

2. 文章中の「数え上げる表現（例：First）」を□で囲みましょう。

3. まとめの文に波線を引きましょう。

■■■ **Model paragraph 2** ■■■

以下、ファストフードと家庭料理の相違点を説明するパラグラフを書きます。

ファストフードと家庭料理

ファストフードと家庭料理にはお互いに大きな違いがある。

相違点1： ファストフードは家庭料理より早い。（時間）

　説明1： ファストフードはお店に行けばすぐに食べられるし、持ち帰りもできる。

　説明2： 家庭料理は、まず材料をお店に買いに行き、家で調理しなければならない。

相違点2： ファストフードは家庭料理よりも安い。（お金）

　説明1： クーポン割引などがあるため、ファストフードは安い値段で買うことができる。

　説明2： 家庭料理はいろいろな材料や調味料が必要であり、電気代やガス代も必要である。

相違点3： 家庭料理はファストフードよりも健康的である。（健康）

　説明1： ファストフードは砂糖や塩、保存料など食品添加物も多く使われている。

　説明2： 家庭料理は新鮮な野菜も使え、砂糖や塩などの量も自分で調節できる。

Fast food vs Home-cooked food

Fast food and home-cooked food (1   ) vastly from each other. (2   ), fast food is "faster" than home-cooked food. You can eat fast food as soon as you get to the shop, or you can take it home. For home-cooking, you first have to buy food at the store and cook it at home. (3   ), fast food is cheaper than home-cooked food. By using (4   ), you can buy fast food at a low price. To cook at home, you need not only various ingredients and (5   ) but also the electricity and gas charges. (6   ), a home-cooked meal is healthier than fast food. Fast food uses a lot of sugar and salt, as well as many (7   ) additives such as (8   ). You can use fresh vegetables and control the amount of sugar and salt if you cook at home.

1. 空欄に適切な語を下の語群から選びましょう。

[First / Second / Third / food / differ / preservatives / coupons / seasonings]

2. トピックセンテンスに下線を引きましょう。

■■■   Vocabulary   ■■■

以下の意味を表す英単語を選び、( )に書きましょう。

1. (   ): the situation of being like something but not exactly the same
2. (   ): having very good things for your body to grow
3. (   ): an illness of humans, animals or plants
4. (   ): costing a lot of money
5. (   ): able to be used or obtained
6. (   ): to be different from something
7. (   ): cooked at home
8. (   ): items that things can be made from
9. (   ): something used to keep food from going bad
10. (   ): one of the foods used to make a particular dish

[home-cooked, expensive, nutritious, ingredient, differ, material, disease, preservative, similarity, available]

Grammar and expressions

1. 以下の日本文に合う英文を書きましょう。

(1) あなたのカメラは私のものより小さい。

_____

(2) ボブ (Bob) は5人の中で最も若い。

_____

(3) 彼女は日本の中で最も人気のある歌手の一人です。

_____

(4) ナオ (Nao) はユキ (Yuki) と同じくらい一生懸命勉強をする。

_____

(5) この机はあの机と同じくらい古い。

_____

2. 適切な文になるように、空欄に当てはまるものを選び記号で答えましょう。

1. I was introduced to her, but we exchanged (　　) a few words.

   A. no more than　　**B.** as many as　　**C.** as good as　　**D.** no less than

2. The people seem (　　) satisfied with their lives.

   A. sooner or later　　**B.** as well as　　**C.** less more　　**D.** more or less

3. We have to hurry. The plane leaves in (　　) two hours.

   A. better than　　**B.** more than　　**C.** less than　　**D.** worse than

4. It's too expensive! We can pay 100 dollars (　　).

   A. at least　　**B.** at worst　　**C.** at most　　**D.** at first

5. I hear Tom's house is near the station. It should be (　　) a five-minute walk from the station.

   A. all better　　**B.** not more than　　**C.** over　　**D.** not less than

Writing exercise

Model paragraph 2で挙げられていないファストフードと家庭料理の相違点を2つ考えて、それぞれ英語1文で書いてみましょう。

・_____

・_____

Unit 3 · Lesson 2

Advantages and Disadvantages

　ものごとには必ず両面性がある。[　　　　　]と[　　　　　]を洗い出すことが重要である。時に、[　　　　]と[　　　　　]は入れ替わることもある。人や状況、課題に応じて、柔軟に考えることも大切である。

[　]に入る日本語を考えてみましょう。

◆ Warm-up questions ◆

1. How long do you usually talk with friends every day?
2. How many emails or messages do you send every day?
3. Which do you like, talking face-to-face or texting?

■■■　Model paragraph 1　■■■

Face-to-face communication

Ways of communication have changed with the rapid development of technology, but face-to-face communication is important. Of course, face-to-face communication has some disadvantages. For example, you must make an appointment to meet with people, including the date, time, and place. Also, you need to pay for transportation to go to the meeting place. On the contrary, face-to-face communication enables you to use not only verbal expression but also body language to express your thoughts or feelings. It is often said that body language speaks louder than words. In addition, you can get responses quickly when you communicate with each other in person. Talking to someone face-to-face is an effective communication style.

【内容理解】

1. 対面コミュニケーションのメリットは（　　　）個、デメリットは（　　　）個、挙げられている。

2. 対面コミュニケーションのメリット・デメリットについて整理してみましょう。

メリット	デメリット

【形式理解】

1. トピックセンテンスに下線を引きましょう。

2. 文章中の「つなぎ表現（例：Of course）」を□で囲みましょう。

3. まとめの文に波線を引きましょう。

Model paragraph 2

Email communication

Email is an important method of communication in modern society. One of the main advantages of email is that you can send messages to others whenever you want. Before sending an email, you can have enough time to think about the content of your email and check it carefully. In addition, email is a free tool of communication except for the cost of your internet connection. You can send many text messages as well as photos, videos, and files. On the other hand, you should be aware that you cannot always contact others immediately by email. If people don't find your message in their inbox, it is hard to tell when you can get a response from them. Sometimes you should be careful when you open an email. When your computer is infected by a virus, there may be trouble with unexpected computer behavior or sudden crashes. As mentioned above, there are some disadvantages, but email is an essential tool of communication.

Unit 3 : L 2

【内容理解】

1. メールコミュニケーションのメリットは（　　）個、デメリットは（　　）個、挙げられている。

2. メールコミュニケーションのメリット・デメリットについて整理してみましょう。

メリット	デメリット

【形式理解】

1. トピックセンテンスに下線を引きましょう。

2. 文章中の「つなぎ表現」を□で囲んでみましょう。

3. まとめの文に波線を引きましょう。

Vocabulary

以下の意味を表す英単語を選び、（　　）に書きましょう。

1. (　　　　　　　　　): an amount of money paid for a particular service

2. (　　　　　　　　　): to be different from something else in size, shape, etc.

3. (　　　　　　　　　): to make it possible for somebody to do something

4. (　　　　　　　　　): a reaction to something that has happened or been said

5. (　　　　　　　　　): meeting someone directly rather than communicating by phone, email, etc.

6. (　　　　　　　　　): at once; straight away; instantly

7. (　　　　　　　　　): knowing about something, a situation or fact

8. (　　　　　　　　　): to pass or spread an illness to a person, an animal or a plant

9. (　　　　　　　　　): the way that somebody acts

10. (　　　　　　　　　): necessary and important

> in person, enable, response, immediately, aware, infect, essential, fee, vary, behavior

1. 以下の日本文に合う英文を書きましょう。

   (1) マイク（Mike）はトム（Tom）の2倍速く走る。

   _____

   (2) アン（Ann）は母親ほど背が高くない。（as を使って）

   _____

   (3) 今日は昨日よりも少し寒い。

   _____

   (4) この川はあの川よりはるかに長い。

   _____

   (5) 彼女はクラスの中で他のどの女子よりも背が高い。（any を使って）

   _____

2. A〜Dの中から、文法的に適切でないものを見つけ、記号で答えましょう。

   1. Either coffee or tea will be fine as farther as I'm concerned. (　　)
              A   B   will   C   D

   2. I don't like it. I dislike not as much the color as the shape. (　　)
                            A   B   C   D

   3. I am not longer a child. It's time to stand on my own feet and make my way in
           A   B   C   D
      the world. (　　)

   4. I didn't like English at first. But, the more I studied it, the most I liked it. (　　)
                          A   B   C   D

   5. You should try to walk as much so possible every day to stay in good health.
                       A   B   C   D
      (　　)

Model paragraph 1で挙げられていない、対面コミュニケーションのメリットとデメリットを1つずつ英語で書いてみましょう。

メリット：_____

デメリット：_____

Unit 3: L 2

35

Unit 3 • Lesson 3

1. What time do you go to bed?
2. How long do you sleep at night?
3. Are you a morning-person or a night-person?

■■■　Model paragraph　■■■

Trains vs Cars

If you live in the city, using trains is a better way to commute than driving a car. First, moving by train is safer than by car. Even if you drive a car carefully, you are more likely to be in an accident than taking a train. Certainly, there are accidents and breakdowns on trains too. However, there are few accidents that cause passengers to get injured or die. Second, moving by train is more punctual than by car. Traffic congestion often occurs on urban roads. If you get into a traffic jam, you cannot predict when you will arrive at your destination. On the other hand, trains are usually on time. Moreover, it is really easy to find out the quickest way to your destination by using an application. In conclusion, trains are more convenient than cars in terms of safety and time accuracy, especially if you are in the city.

【形式理解】

1. トピックセンテンスに下線を引きましょう。
2. 文章中の「つなぎ表現」を□で囲みましょう。
3. まとめの文に波線を引きましょう。

Topic **What are the advantages and disadvantages of a morning-person or a night-person?**

Brainstorm ●

朝型と夜型のメリットとデメリットについて日本語で書いてみましょう。

	メリット	デメリット
朝型		
夜型		

Outline ●

朝型か夜型のどちらかを選んで、メリットとデメリットについてのパラグラフのアウトラインを作成しましょう。

トピックセンテンス: _____

メリット: _____

　説明: _____

デメリット: _____

　説明: _____

まとめ: _____

Unit 3 : L 3

37

Your paragraph

アウトラインをもとに、80語以上のパラグラフを書きましょう。

Peer feedback ● クラスメイトとパラグラフを交換し確認しましょう。

1. トピックセンテンスはありますか？　「はい」・「いいえ」

2. どのようなポイントが書かれていますか？　すべて書いてみましょう。

・ _____

・ _____

3. つなぎの表現は入っていますか？
　「はい」→ 使われている表現を書いてみましょう。
　「いいえ」→ つなぎの表現を提案してみましょう。

・ _____

4. まとめの文はありますか？　「はい」・「いいえ」

5. パラグラフの内容はすべて分かりましたか？
　「はい」
　「いいえ」→ どこが分かりませんでしたか？

・ _____

6. パラグラフの良い点を1つ挙げましょう。

・ _____

Revise ● 上のコメントをもとに、自分のパラグラフを修正しましょう。

Unit 4

Cause / Effect Paragraph

What is a Cause / Effect Paragraph?

　物事が起こるには「　　　　」がある。Cause / effect paragraphは、物事の「　　　　」もしくは「　　　　」について書くパラグラフである。時には両方を書く場合もある。大学の課題では、学生自身で因果関係について検討することが必要になる場合が多い。

[　]に入る日本語を考えてみましょう。

◆ Warm-up questions ◆

1. How often do you use your cell phone?
2. For what do you most use your cell phone?
3. How much do you think is the appropriate price for cell phone per month?

> **Background:** Cell phone addiction is a social problem. It is defined as people's dependency on devices at the cost of harming relationships as well as physical and psychological health. In particular, dependency on Social Networking Services (SNS) is a problem familiar to many university students.

● ある事象について議論する際に、はじめに定義づけることが必要になることがあります。この背景の説明にある表現「it is defined as ...」(〜と定義される)などは便利な表現です。

Model paragraph 1

SNS addiction

Three factors cause SNS addiction among young people. First, the convenience of SNS leads to frequent use. SNS allows people to communicate anytime and anywhere with an unlimited number of people free of charge. Second, SNS has become the main means of sending and receiving information, from class assignments to political news. As a result, people feel a sense of security when they stay on SNS to obtain necessary information and connect with society. Finally, young people often use SNS for no particular reason. They use it to kill time, playing games and texting with friends, and this behavior leads to the development of SNS dependency. For these reasons, many young people are addicted to SNS.

【内容理解】

1. SNS中毒の原因は、（　　　　）個ある。

2. 1つ目の原因は（　　　　　　　　　　　　　　　　　　　　　　　　　　　　）

3. 2つ目の原因は（　　　　　　　　　　　　　　　　　　　　　　　　　　　　）

4. 3つ目の原因は（　　　　　　　　　　　　　　　　　　　　　　　　　　　　）

【形式理解】

1. トピックセンテンスに下線を引きましょう。

2. 1つ目、2つ目、3つ目の原因を導く表現を□で囲みましょう。

3. まとめの文があれば波線を引きましょう。

■■■　Model paragraph 2　■■■

以下、長寿の原因を説明するパラグラフを書きます。空欄に適切な語句を下の語群から選びましょう。

長寿

原因1：医療の発展により、過去には治療できなかった病気を治すことが可能となった。

　説明・例1：新しい薬が開発され、安価で手に入る。

　説明・例2：技術の進歩によって、患者に痛みをもたらすことなく、難しい病気に対応できる。

原因2：健康への意識が向上した。

　説明・例1：政府の広報活動のおかげで、適度な運動とバランスの良い食事が長寿の鍵であると認知されている。

　説明・例2：健康診断を定期的に受けて、病気を予防している。

Longer life

People are living longer nowadays for (1　　　　　　　　). (2　　　　　　　　) is medical advancements that make it possible to cure many diseases that were untreatable (3　　　　　　　　). New drugs have been (4　　　　　　　　) and are available at affordable prices. Technological progress has also contributed to the ability to treat difficult diseases without causing (5　　　　　　　　) much pain. (6　　　　　　　　) is people's increased awareness of health. (7　　　　　　　　) the government's promotional efforts, people know that appropriate exercise and well-balanced diets are the keys to a long, healthy life. (8   ), people have regular health checkups to (9   ) illnesses and detect diseases early. (10   ), these are the reasons why people tend to live for a long time now.

> The first cause / developed / prevent / two main reasons / In conclusion / The second cause / patients / Thanks to / in the past / In addition

Vocabulary

以下の意味を表す単語を選び、(　)に書きましょう。

1. (　　　　　　　　　): to give something, especially money or support, to help achieve something

2. (　　　　　　　　　): an occasion or situation that makes it possible to do something that you want to do

3. (　　　　　　　　　): all the people living in a particular country, area, or place

4. (　　　　　　　　　): a person who lives or has their home in a place

5. (　　　　　　　　　): a large number or amount of something in the same place

6. (　　　　　　　　　): an inability to stop doing or using something, especially something harmful

7. (　　　　　　　　　): to stop something from happening or someone from doing something

8. (　　　　　　　　　): to say what the meaning of something, especially a word, is

9. (　　　　　　　　　): suitable or right for a particular situation or occasion

10. (　　　　　　　　　): to pull or draw someone or something toward them, by the qualities they have

> resident, concentration, population, addiction, prevent, opportunity, define, appropriate, attract, contribute

44

■原因を示す表現と用法

接続詞	for, as, because, since
前置詞句	because of, due to, as a result of
動詞	cause, result, lead
副詞（句）	therefore, as a result

1. （　）に入る適切な語を、上の表から選びましょう。正解が一つとは限りません。

> ### Population concentration
>
> While Japan's population is decreasing, the number of residents in major cities is increasing. First, better job opportunities (**1**　　　　) people to major cities. (**2**　　　　) these people remain in the cities even after they marry and have children, the population of major cities is continually increasing. When more people live in a city, the city is then capable of providing better infrastructure. (**3**　　　　), the city becomes more convenient and attracts even more people.

2. 適切な文になるように、空欄に当てはまるものを選び記号で答えましょう。

1. The traffic accident (　) many injured people.

     A. made up for　　**B.** got off　　**C.** resulted in　　**D.** suffered from

2. We often have a difference of opinion, but it doesn't (　) our relationship.

     A. affect　　**B.** expect　　**C.** follow　　**D.** attracts

3. A small error here can (　) a serious accident later.

     A. lead to　　**B.** take over　　**C.** look for　　**D.** put on

4. Her broken wrist (　) a fall when she played soccer after school.

     A. brought about　　**B.** depended on　　**C.** thought of　　**D.** resulted from

5. My lack of English (　) me from communicating with the people in the country I visited.

     A. took away　　**B.** prevented　　**C.** made　　**D.** heard

Unit 4 : L 1

3. A～Dの中から、文法的に適切でないものを見つけ、記号で答えましょう。

1. Strong sunlight will <u>cause</u> this cloth <u>turn</u> color. You should <u>keep</u> it in a room
_A _B _C
<u>with</u> no direct sunlight. (　　)
_D

2. Playing tennis <u>allows</u> me <u>putting</u> my <u>work</u> out of my mind <u>for</u> an afternoon. (　　)
_A _B _C _D

3. These features <u>enable</u> a product <u>to</u> be <u>producing</u> rapidly and <u>economically</u>. (　　)
_A _B _C _D

4. The worldwide inflation <u>has forced</u> us <u>to give</u> up our <u>plans</u> <u>to buying</u> a new
_A _B _C _D
house. (　　)

5. I <u>hope</u> this medicine <u>will make</u> me <u>to feel</u> a little <u>better</u>. (　　)
_A _B _C _D

■ ■ ■　Writing exercise　■ ■ ■

少子高齢化の原因を2つ考えて、それぞれ英語1文で書いてみましょう。

原因1：＿＿＿＿＿＿＿＿＿＿＿＿＿＿＿＿＿＿＿＿＿＿＿＿＿＿＿＿＿＿＿＿＿＿＿＿

原因2：＿＿＿＿＿＿＿＿＿＿＿＿＿＿＿＿＿＿＿＿＿＿＿＿＿＿＿＿＿＿＿＿＿＿＿＿

Unit 4 • Lesson 2

◆ **Warm-up questions** ◆

1. What are some manners when using cell phones?
2. Do you use your cell phone during meals?
3. Have you had any problems with your cell phone?

■■■　　Model paragraph 1　　■■■

Effects of SNS

[   ]. Firstly, young people easily become addicted to SNS. They feel anxious if they are not checking messages. Secondly, people lose the ability to communicate in person because they are accustomed to talking online. This is especially a problem for young people who cannot develop the social skills necessary to make friends and work with others. Lastly, SNS harms physical health. People have weak eyesight and stiff necks due to long periods of using cell phones, and poor posture is also becoming a problem. The advancement of communication technology and applications makes our lives convenient, but we must be careful not to become addicted.

【内容理解】

1. SNS中毒の影響は、(　　　　)個ある。
2. 1つ目の影響は (   )
3. 2つ目の影響は (   )
4. 3つ目の影響は (   )

【形式理解】

1. [　　　]に適切なトピックセンテンスを書きましょう。
2. 1つ目、2つ目、3つ目の原因を導く表現を□で囲みましょう。
3. まとめの文があれば波線を引きましょう。

Unit 4: L 2

47

Model paragraph 2

以下、温暖化の影響を説明するパラグラフを書きます。空欄に適切な語句を下の語群から選びましょう。

温暖化

影響1：極地の氷が解けて海面が上昇する。

　説明・例1：浸水する土地が出てくる。

　説明・例2：浸水した土地の住民は住む場所がなくなる。

影響2：生態系が変化する。

　説明・例1：日本には見られなかった魚や虫が出てくる。

　説明・例2：日本にいた魚や虫がいなくなり始め、経済に影響を及ぼす。

Global warming

Global warming has a significant (1 　　　　　) on our lives and the environment. (2 　　　　), warm temperatures are melting glaciers on the Earth, so the sea levels are (3 　　　). (4 　　　), land will sink below the sea. People on submerged land will lose their homes. (5 　　　), the ecosystem will also be affected. We now see fish and insects that did not live in Japan before, and some fish and insects that have always lived in Japan are beginning to disappear. Because of this, the country's agricultural and fishing industries will be (6 　　　), and the economy will suffer. Global warming is not a problem we can (7 　　　).

[effect / Consequently / Second / affected / ignore / rising / First]

Vocabulary

以下の意味を表す単語を選び、（　）に書きましょう。

1. (　　　　　): to cause someone to change a behavior, belief, or opinion, or to cause something to be changed
2. (　　　　　): worried and nervous
3. (　　　　　): as a result
4. (　　　　　): to make someone want to do something well
5. (　　　　　): important or noticeable
6. (　　　　　): to examine or look for the similarity / difference between two or more things

48

7. (   ): the measured amount of heat in a place or in the body

8. (   ): to intentionally not listen or give attention to

9. (   ): the situation within which something exists or happens, and that can help explain it

10. (   ): a fact or situation that influences the result of something

> compare, consequently, ignore, anxious, context, significant, temperature, influence, factor, motivate

Grammar and expressions

■結果を示す表現と用法

接続詞	so, for, as, because, since
前置詞句	because of, due to, as a result of
動詞	cause, result, follow, affect, influence
副詞 (句)	therefore, as a result, consequently

1. （ ）に入る適切な語を、上の表から選びましょう。正解が一つとは限りません。

> **Good teachers**
>
> It is important to meet good teachers when we are children (1   ) they can influence how young people think about themselves and their futures. Good teachers can motivate young people to study hard to become better adults. These teachers can also offer specific advice about career paths based on students' academic performance and personalities. In fact, many high school students say that they choose their university and major (2   ) their teachers' advice. (3   ), we can suggest that having a good teacher is an important success factor.

2. 適切な文になるように、空欄に当てはまるものを選び記号で答えましょう。

1. (   ) heavy rain, we had to cancel the picnic.

   A. Thanks to   **B.** According to   **C.** In order to   **D.** Because of

2. This is a difficult theme. (   ), I will begin by defining a few terms.

   A. Therefore   **B.** In addition   **C.** Owing to   **D.** Regarding

3. (   ) a lack of rain, the river dried up.

   A. Thus   **B.** Speaking of   **C.** As to   **D.** Due to

Unit 4: L 4-2

49

4. My son has a good memory, and (　　　) does well in all his subjects.

    A. consequently   **B.** namely   **C.** similarly   **D.** in contrast

5. He made great efforts. (　　　), he succeeded in his job.

    A. By contrast   **B.** Moreover   **C.** As a result   **D.** Furthermore

3. A～Dの中から、文法的に適切でないものを見つけ、記号で答えましょう。

                                A   B   C
1. Our college's football team is sure to win, then the other side has clearly lost
   D
   its fighting spirit. (　　　)

                               A   B
2. A world-famous scientist is going to come to Tokyo next week, as you will be
         C   D
   able to meet him there. (　　　)

   A   B   C   D
3. For I walk a lot to go to school, I have to buy at least five pairs of shoes every

   year. (　　　)

   A   B   C
4. There was something wrong with my computer today, however I was unable to
   D
   use it. (　　　)

                       A   B   C   D
5. Researchers are studying animals' eyes so they hold some keys to biological

   history. (　　　)

■■■　Writing exercise　■■■

キャッシュレス化の影響を2つ考えて、それぞれ英語1文で書いてみましょう。

影響1：...

影響2：...

◆ Warm-up questions ◆

1. Has your sleeping hour changed since you became a university student? If yes, how?
2. Do you think it is important for a person to sleep enough? Why?
3. What is important for good health?

■■■ Model paragraph ■■■

Cashless society

A cashless society can have several effects on our lives. First, any financial transactions will become very convenient. Since all transactions will be completed electronically, we will not need to withdraw cash, and shops will not have to manage it. In addition, the danger of robbery will decrease because people will not carry cash. At the same time, if we do not actually see money, it will be easy for us to overspend and lose track of our budgets. More people could go bankrupt due to cashless payment systems. Another danger is personal information leaks online and system hacking. In summary, a cashless society can have both positive and negative effects.

1. トピックセンテンスに下線を引きましょう。
2. まとめの文に波線を引きましょう。
3. cause / effect paragraphを示唆する表現を□で囲みましょう。

■■■ Paragraph writing ■■■

Topic **What are the causes / effects of lack of sleep among university students?**

Brainstorm ●

● 大学生の睡眠不足の原因を考えてみましょう。

● 睡眠不足による影響を考えてみましょう。

原因・影響のどちらかを選んで、アウトラインを作成しましょう。

トピックセンテンス：

原因／影響 1：

　説明（例）：

原因／影響 2：

　説明（例）：

まとめ：

Your paragraph

アウトラインをもとに、80語以上のパラグラフを書きましょう。タイトルもつけましょう。

Peer feedback ● クラスメイトとパラグラフを交換し確認しましょう。

1. トピックセンテンスはありますか？　　「はい」・「いいえ」

2. どのようなポイントが書かれていますか？　すべて書いてみましょう。

・_____

・_____

3. つなぎの表現は入っていますか？

「はい」→ 使われている表現を書いてみましょう。

「いいえ」→ つなぎの表現を提案してみましょう。

・_____

4. まとめの文はありますか？　　「はい」・「いいえ」

5. パラグラフの内容はすべて分かりましたか？

「はい」

「いいえ」→ どこが分かりませんでしたか？

・_____

6. パラグラフの良い点を1つ挙げましょう。

・_____

Revise ● 上のコメントをもとに、自分のパラグラフを修正しましょう。

Unit 5

Opinion Paragraph

Unit 5 • Lesson 1

What's an Opinion Paragraph?

Opinion Paragraph：ある話題について、賛成・反対などの［　　　］を述べる

●使用例：レポート、エッセイ、［　　　］、社説など

●言語的特徴：自分の立場を［　　　］に書く。主張の根拠となる［　　　］を導く表現が使われる。

［　］に入る日本語を考えてみましょう。

◆ Warm-up questions ◆

1. How many tests have you taken outside the class?
2. What kind of test did you take last?
3. Why do you think the tests are needed?

Background: Japanese students take many kinds of tests from elementary to high school. Among them, 15-year-old students take an international academic test called PISA every three years. Japanese people have different opinions on taking PISA.

※PISA…OECD加盟国を中心に、3年ごとに実施される15歳児の学習到達度調査。

Model paragraph 1

Are you for or against taking the PISA test?

I agree that students should take the test. I have two reasons for this. First, the Japanese government can find out the strong and weak points of its education policies. In fact, the 2003 results of PISA showed that Japan dropped from the world's top ranks. After that, the Japanese government decided to discontinue its 'relaxed' method of education called "Yutori Kyouiku." Second, schools can show that their teaching methods are effective. The PISA 2015 results revealed that Japanese students ranked second in science, eighth in reading, and fifth in math among 72 countries and regions. I believe this shows as evidence of the huge efforts made by teachers.

【内容理解】 Kaoriが書いた左の文章を読んで、以下の問いに答えましょう。

1. KaoriはPISAに（ 賛成 ・ 反対 ）

2. 1つ目の理由は（ 　　　　　　　　　　　　　　　　　　　　　　　　　　　）

→ それを説明する例は（ 　　　　　　　　　　　　　　　　　　　　　　　　）

3. 2つ目の理由は（ 　　　　　　　　　　　　　　　　　　　　　　　　　　　）

→ それを説明する例は（ 　　　　　　　　　　　　　　　　　　　　　　　　）

【形式理解】

1. 理由が2つあることを示す文に下線を引きましょう。

2. 1つ目と2つ目の理由を導く表現を□で囲みましょう。

3. 1つ目と2つ目の理由を説明する文に波線を引きましょう。

■■■　Model paragraph 2　■■■

以下の質問についてYukiは賛成しています。空欄にあてはまる語句を語群から選びましょう。

Do you agree that students should take part
in club activities at university?

理由1： 体育会系の部活動に入ると、健康を維持することができる。
　説明・例： 実際、大学では週に1度しか体育の授業がない。
　　　　　　高校の時には週に2〜3回、体育の時間があった。
理由2： 他学部や他大学の友人をたくさん作ることができる。
　説明・例： 部活動にはさまざまな学部の人が参加している。
　　　　　　大学では他学部の学生と一緒の授業を受ける機会があまり多くない。
　　　　　　さらに、他大学の学生と出会う機会はほとんどない。

Club activities for university students

I think that students should (1　　　　　　　) club activities at university. I have (2　　　　　). (3　　　　　　　), they can (4　　　　　) when they are in a sport club. (5　　　　　), students have only one lesson for exercise a week at university. When they were high school students, they had physical education lessons (6　　　　　) a week. (7　　　　　　), they can (8　　　　　) from different departments or universities in a club. In a university, students don't (9　　　　　) to take the same lessons with students from other departments. Moreover, they (10　　　　　) to meet students from other universities.

Vocabulary

以下の意味を表す動詞を選び、（　）に書きましょう。

1. (　　　　　　　　　): to have a particular idea or opinion about something
2. (　　　　　　　　　): to understand or become aware of a particular fact
3. (　　　　　　　　　): to feel certain that something is true
4. (　　　　　　　　　): to put forward an idea or a plan for people to think about
5. (　　　　　　　　　): (formal) to suggest an idea or a plan for people to think about
6. (　　　　　　　　　): to speak or tell somebody something, using words
7. (　　　　　　　　　): to formally write or say something, especially in a careful and clear way
8. (　　　　　　　　　): to decide or believe something as a result of what you have heard or seen
9. (　　　　　　　　　): to suggest that something is true without saying so directly
10. (　　　　　　　　　): to make something clear

[state, imply, believe, think, propose, realize, suggest, say, conclude, show]

Grammar and expressions

1. 適切な文になるように、空欄に当てはまるものを選び記号で答えましょう。

1. My teacher suggested that I (　　) two more reports before I graduated from university.

        A. write   **B.** wrote   **C.** written   **D.** had written

2. The bus-stop sign stated that the bus (　　) making five stops before arriving at the City Museum.

        A. will   **B.** will be   **C.** was to   **D.** would be

3. I proposed that we (　　) Steve's idea because it sounded so useful for society as a whole.

      A. accept   **B.** accepted   **C.** accepting   **D.** to accept

4. It (　　) dark by the time we arrive.

      A. is   **B.** got   **C.** will be   **D.** being

5. They will start to write a report as soon as they (　　) the market research.

      A. finished   **B.** finish   **C.** finishing   **D.** will finish

2. A～Dの中から、文法的に適切でないものを見つけ、記号で答えましょう。

1. Today's weather forecast says[A] that it will be[B] fine tomorrow. Do you think[C] that she comes[D] camping? (　　)

2. It is[A] reported that the family could[B] move into the apartment after the renovation is[C] finished[D]. (　　)

3. Mr. Hasegawa is[A] planning[B] to pick up[C] his wife when she will arrive[D] at Narita International Airport. (　　)

4. The students requested[A] that they be[B] given[C] another week to finishing[D] their homework. (　　)

5. If you are[A] ill or have[B] other problems, I suggested[C] you take[D] a couple of weeks off. (　　)

■ ■ ■　　　**Writing exercise**　　　■ ■ ■

PISAのような国際学習到達度調査のメリットとその理由について英語で一文ずつ書いてみましょう。

調査のメリット：＿＿＿＿＿＿＿＿＿＿＿＿＿＿＿＿＿＿＿＿＿＿＿＿＿＿＿＿＿

理由：＿＿＿＿＿＿＿＿＿＿＿＿＿＿＿＿＿＿＿＿＿＿＿＿＿＿＿＿＿＿＿＿＿＿

Unit 5: L 1

Unit 5 • Lesson 2

◆ Warm-up questions ◆

1. What club activities did you join in junior high school and high school?
2. How many club activities does your university have?
3. Do you take part in club activities at university? Why / Why not?

Model paragraph 1

Do you agree to take part in PISA?

Although there are many good points in taking PISA, I think that people should be careful of using the results of PISA for the following two reasons. First, the test can only measure a narrow range of knowledge and skills. It cannot measure basic skills such as communication and using computers or important aspects of human nature such as morality and creativity. These abilities are necessary for academic success in today's global society. Second, teachers feel too much pressure from the results of PISA. As a result, they may teach to the tests and lose their originality. Teachers use many unique ways to bring up their students. For example, teachers in Japan visit students' homes to get a better understanding of their family. However, teachers will not take time doing such work when they are evaluated mainly by the results of PISA.

【内容理解】Naokiが書いた上の文章を読んで、以下の問いに答えましょう。

1. NaokiはPISAに（　賛成　・　反対　）

2. 1つ目の理由は（　　　　　　　　　　　　　　　　　　　　　　　　　　　　　　）
→　それを説明する例は（　　　　　　　　　　　　　　　　　　　　　　　　　　　　）

3. 2つ目の理由は（　　　　　　　　　　　　　　　　　　　　　　　　　　　　　　　）
→　それを説明する例は（　　　　　　　　　　　　　　　　　　　　　　　　　　　　）

【形式理解】

1. 賛成または反対を表す部分に下線を引きましょう。
2. 理由が2つあることを示す表現を□で囲みましょう。
3. 1つ目と2つ目の理由を説明する文に波線を引きましょう。

以下の質問についてChiekoは反対しています。空欄にあてはまる語句を語群から選びましょう。

Do you agree that students should take part in club activities at university?

理由1：大学生は自分の好きな時間に体を動かすことができる。

　説明・例：家の近くのスポーツジムに入会することができる年齢である。

　　　　　スポーツジムはほとんどが24時間営業である。

　　　　　ほとんどすべての大学に体育館があり、学生は無料で利用できる。

理由2：アルバイトで他学部や他大学の友人を作ることができる。

　説明・例：他学部や他大学の学生だけでなく、大人とも知り合うことができる。

　　　　　一生懸命働けば、大学卒業後にそのまま就職できるかもしれない。

Club activities for university students

I (1　　　　　) that students should take part in club activities at university for the (2　　　　　). (3　　　　　), university students can exercise any time they like. They are old (4　　　　　) join a private gym near their house. Most of the gyms are open (5　　　　　). Moreover, almost all universities have their own gyms on campus. Students can use them (6　　　　　). (7　　　　　), university students can make friends from different departments or universities when they (8　　　　　). They can meet (9　　　　　) but also professionals. If they work hard at the workplace, they may get some job opportunities after they (10　　　　　) university.

not only students / Second / following two reasons / First / enough to / 24 hours a day / work part-time / for free / disagree / graduate from

Unit 5 : L 2

61

以下の語句を1〜3の使い方に分類し、それぞれ例文を作ってみましょう。

> although, in spite of, even though, despite,
> still, nonetheless, however, nevertheless, regardless of

1. 接続詞：文と文をつなぐ（＿＿＿＿＿＿＿＿＿＿＿＿ , ＿＿＿＿＿＿＿＿＿＿＿＿ ）

   例文 ＿＿＿＿＿＿＿＿＿＿＿＿＿＿＿＿＿＿＿＿＿＿＿＿＿＿＿＿＿

2. 前置詞（句）：名詞の前に置く（＿＿＿＿＿＿ , ＿＿＿＿＿＿ , ＿＿＿＿＿＿ ）

   例文 ＿＿＿＿＿＿＿＿＿＿＿＿＿＿＿＿＿＿＿＿＿＿＿＿＿＿＿＿＿

3. 副詞：単独で使う（＿＿＿＿＿ , ＿＿＿＿＿ , ＿＿＿＿＿ , ＿＿＿＿＿ ）

   例文 ＿＿＿＿＿＿＿＿＿＿＿＿＿＿＿＿＿＿＿＿＿＿＿＿＿＿＿＿＿

1. 適切な文になるように、空欄に当てはまるものを選び記号で答えましょう。

   1. Did you go to university today (　　) it is a Sunday?

      A. although　　**B.** in spite of　　**C.** despite　　**D.** however

   2. (　　) all our planning, we decided not to go after all.

      A. nonetheless　　**B.** still　　**C.** yet　　**D.** despite

   3. "It sounds true, but (　　), what you say is an attempt to excuse yourself."
      "No, it's true."

      A. in spite of　　**B.** even though　　**C.** nevertheless　　**D.** regardless of

   4. Tom has a lot of good ideas (　　) he may not always express them.

      A. even though　　**B.** still　　**C.** despite　　**D.** nonetheless

   5. He was once a famous clothing designer. In recent years, (　　), his designs have become old-fashioned.

      A. regardless of　　**B.** however　　**C.** in spite of　　**D.** although

2. A〜Dの中から、文法的に適切でないものを見つけ、記号で答えましょう。

   1. The role of the teachers was to give students much information 50 years ago.
      A

B   C   D

Despite, current teachers have to help students find information by themselves. ( )

     A   B   C   D

2. Please reply regardless of whether or not you plan to participating. ( )

   A   B   C   D

3. However we found the road out of the mountain, we were still not out of

danger. ( )

          A   B   C

4. Takeshi got angry that he was not chosen as a project leader nonetheless his

      D

five years of hard work. ( )

          A   B

5. We didn't know much about the importance of sleep for our health. In recent

      C   D

years, although, many researchers have noticed it. ( )

■ ■ ■   **Writing exercise**   ■ ■ ■

PISAのような国際学習到達度調査のデメリットとその理由について英語で一文ずつ書いてみましょう。

調査のデメリット：＿＿＿＿＿＿＿＿＿＿＿＿＿＿＿＿＿＿＿＿＿＿＿＿＿＿＿＿＿＿＿

理由：＿＿＿＿＿＿＿＿＿＿＿＿＿＿＿＿＿＿＿＿＿＿＿＿＿＿＿＿＿＿＿＿＿＿＿＿＿

Unit 5 • Lesson 3

1. What did you eat for lunch in high school?
2. What did you eat for lunch yesterday?
3. How much do you think is the appropriate price for lunch?

Model paragraph

School lunch at junior high schools

I think that junior high schools should provide lunches for the following two reasons. First, students can have well-balanced meals at a low cost. For example, in Japan, the calories of school lunch menus are strictly calculated by experts, and each meal only costs 200 yen. Second, students can learn about local food sources. Most school lunches use local ingredients such as fish, meat, and vegetables. Students can enjoy their meals with their classmates too. These experiences can lead students to become more interested in their hometown and local food production. These are the reasons why I think school lunches should be provided at junior high schools.

Yokoが書いた上の文章を読んで、以下の問いに答えましょう。

1. Yokoは中学校の給食に（　賛成　・　反対　）
2. まとめの文に下線を引きましょう。

Paragraph writing

Topic **Do you agree that university students should bring packed lunches?**

Brainstorm ●

P. 67の資料を参考にして、自分の意見を考えてみましょう。

_____

_____

_____

_____

_____

_____

Outline ●

パラグラフのアウトラインを作成しましょう。

トピックセンテンス：	
理由1：	
説明（例）：	
理由2：	
説明（例）：	
まとめ：	

Your paragraph

アウトラインをもとに、80語以上のパラグラフを書きましょう。

_____

_____

_____

_____

_____

_____

_____

_____

_____

_____

_____

_____

_____

_____

_____

_____

Peer feedback ● クラスメイトとパラグラフを交換し確認しましょう。

1. トピックセンテンスはありますか？　　「はい」・「いいえ」

2. どのようなポイントが書かれていますか？　すべて書いてみましょう。

　　　・_____

　　　・_____

3. つなぎの表現は入っていますか？

　　　「はい」→ 使われている表現を書いてみましょう。

　　　「いいえ」→ つなぎの表現を提案してみましょう。

　　　・_____

4. まとめの文はありますか？　　「はい」・「いいえ」

5. パラグラフの内容はすべて分かりましたか？

　　　「はい」

　　　「いいえ」→ どこが分かりませんでしたか？

　　　・_____

6. パラグラフの良い点を1つ挙げましょう。

　　　・_____

Revise ● 上のコメントをもとに、自分のパラグラフを修正しましょう。

資　料：大学生等の食環境と食行動、食への関心に関する調査

（平成26年10月　農林水産省　関東農政局）

《平日の昼食の取り方》

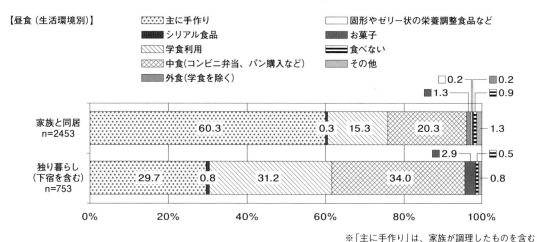

※「主に手作り」は、家族が調理したものを含む

《食生活を改善したいと思う》

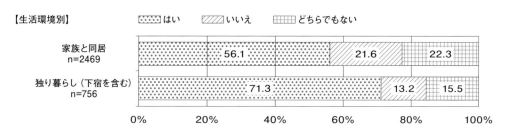

《食費はできるだけ切り詰めたい》

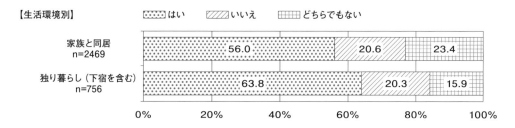

《料理をすることが好き》

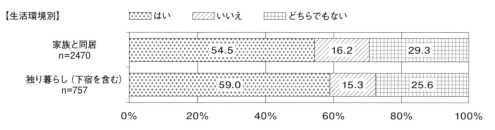

Unit 6

Toward Writing a 300-Word Essay

　このユニットでは、今までに学習したことを応用して、300語程度のエッセイを書くことを目指します。エッセイとは、いくつかのパラグラフからなるまとまりのある文章です。各パラグラフの基本的な型は同じです。最初にトピックセンテンスを書き、それを支持する文を繋げます。パラグラフが長くなる場合には、最後にまとめのセンテンスがあると、より分かりやすくなるでしょう。

　エッセイ全体の構成は、序論（Introduction）・本論（Body）・結論（Conclusion）の3つから成り立っています。序論（1パラグラフ）では、トピックの背景とエッセイでの主張を述べ、本論（2～3パラグラフ）では、説明などの詳細を加えながら主張を展開します。結論（1パラグラフ）は、本論で述べたことを要約し、まとめとします。

■■■　　　　　　　　　**Model essay**　　　　　　　　　■■■

The right to choose

1　　Many junior and high schools in Japan have uniforms for their students. School uniforms are supposed to help students focus on their studies rather than their clothes. Uniforms serve as symbols to unite and discipline students. In addition, parents do not have to spend money on clothes. Uniforms are economical and fair to students of different family backgrounds. For these reasons, school uniforms are widely supported. However, I believe enforcing school uniforms is not helpful for students for two main reasons.

2　　First, school uniforms restrict freedom of expression. The right to choose one's clothing should belong to students, not the school. Some girls may prefer to wear pants and boots to express themselves. By not granting a choice, schools take away freedom of expression, a basic human right. Individual freedom should be given priority over any other potential benefits.

3　　Second, school uniforms are not functional. In the current strange climate, we may need to have clothes that can be easily adapted to the weather, and body temperature differs from person to person. School uniforms do not offer a choice in adapting to environments, including air-conditioned rooms. Additionally, school uniforms can prevent active young students from moving easily and engaging in different social, academic, and sports activities. Students should have the ability to choose their clothing for functional purposes.

4　　In conclusion, it is not beneficial for students to be obliged to wear school uniforms. Students should be given the rights to express themselves and choose functional clothing. Even with these rights and choices, students can study effectively. People may be accustomed to school uniforms in Japan, but they must realize the disadvantages of these outfits and allow students to choose their own clothing.

上のエッセイを読み、内容を理解してから各パートを詳しく見ていきましょう。

1 序論

　最初にトピックの背景を書き、最後に自分の主張を述べます。下の図のように逆三角形のイメージです。最後の自分の主張は**主題文 (thesis statement)** と呼ばれ、エッセイではとても重要な役割を持ちます。自分の意見を述べるエッセイでは、ここに自分の立場 (賛成・反対) を書きます。

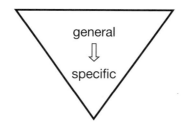

general
⇩
specific

1.　このエッセイのトピックは何ですか。

2.　このエッセイの主題文はどこですか。下線を引き、日本語に訳しましょう。

2 本論

　本論では、主題文で述べた主張に対しての理由や根拠を具体的に展開していきます。本論の各パラグラフのはじめにトピックセンテンスを書き、続けて支持文を展開します。First, Second などの「つなぎ表現」を入れて、読みやすくします。支持文では、具体的な説明や例、データを挙げます。

1.　第2パラグラフのトピックセンテンスに下線を引き、日本語に訳しましょう。

2.　第3パラグラフのトピックセンテンスに下線を引き、日本語に訳しましょう。

Unit 6

③ 結論

　結論部分では、序論で述べた主題文と本論で述べた主なポイントを言い換えてまとめます。結論で新しいアイディアを入れてはいけませんが、トピックに関連した今後の予測や提案をすることは可能です。結論のパラグラフはIn conclusion, In summaryなどいう表現ではじめると良いでしょう。

主題文が言い換えられている結論パラグラフのトピックスセンテンスに下線を引き、日本語に訳しましょう。

Essay writing

Topic

What do you think about the following statement?
"Studying in groups is better than studying alone."

Brainstorm ●

　自分の経験や聞いたことを振り返りながら、効果的な勉強法について思いついたことを日本語で書きましょう。

アウトラインを書きましょう。本論のところには、具体例や詳細な説明を加えましょう。

●序論

（背景）

（主題文）

●本論1

（トピックセンテンス）

（説明・具体例）

●本論2

（トピックセンテンス）

（説明・具体例）

●結論

（主題文の言い換え）

Your essay

アウトラインをもとに、250語以上のエッセイを書きましょう。

Revise ●

エッセイは読み返して見直し、修正をすることがとても大切です。以下のチェックリストを活用し、完成版を作成しましょう。

Checklist

☐ 序論に背景と主題文が書かれている。

☐ 本論の各パラグラフにトピックセンテンスがある。

☐ 本論の各パラグラフには、具体的な例や説明がある。

☐ 結論が本論で書かれたことのまとめとなっている。

☐ 各パラグラフに「つなぎ表現」が使われている。

☐ 文法・語彙・スペルの誤りがない。

はじめてのアカデミックライティング

検印省略	© 2020 年 1 月 31 日　初 版 発 行
	2022 年 9 月 1 日　第 2 刷 発 行

監修者	田 地 野　　彰
編著者	マ ス ワ ナ　紗 矢 子
	加 藤　　由 崇
	渡　　　寛 法
	山 田　　　浩
発行者	原　　雅 久
発行所	株式会社　朝 日 出 版 社

101-0065　東京都千代田区西神田 3-3-5
電話　東京　03-3239-0271
FAX　東京　03-3239-0479
e-mail　text-e@asahipress.com
振替口座　00140-2-46008
組版／ease　製版／錦明印刷

乱丁、落丁本はお取り替えいたします。
ISBN978-4-255-15648-4